Peter Brook

Born in London in 1925, Peter Brook attended Magdalen College, Oxford, and by 1946 was already directing in Stratford (*Love's Labour's Lost*) and London (*Huis Clos*). The fifty or so remarkable productions which followed include Anouilh's *Ring Round the Moon* with Paul Scofield and Whiting's *A Penny for a Song* (1951), *Titus Andronicus* with Olivier and Brook's own music and designs (1955), T.S. Eliot's *The Family Reunion* and Arthur Miller's *A View from the Bridge* (1956), the musical *Irma la Douce* and Dürrenmatt's *The Visit* (1958), *King Lear* with Scofield (1962), *The Physicists* in London and *Serjeant Musgrave's Dance* in Paris (1963), Peter Weiss's *Marat/Sade* (1964), *US* (1966), Seneca's *Oedipus* with Gielgud for the National (1968) and *A Midsummer Night's Dream* for the RSC (1970).

After founding what is now called the Centre International de Créations Théâtrales at the Bouffes du Nord in Paris, Brook mounted *Orghast* in Iran in 1971, a tour of Africa in 1972 – out of which evolved *The Conference of the Birds* – *Timon of Athens* in 1974, *The Ik* (1975), *Ubu* (1977), *The Cherry Orchard* (1981) and *The Mahabharata* (1985). His most recent theatre work includes *The Man Who*, *Qui est là?* and Beckett's *Oh les beaux jours!*

Among his opera productions are *The Marriage of Figaro* and *Boris Godunov* at Covent Garden and *Faust* and *Eugene Onegin* at the Met. His films include *Moderato Cantabile* (1960), *Lord of the Flies* (1963), *King Lear* (1970), *Meetings with Remarkable Men* (1979) and *The Mahabharata* (1989). His first book, *The Empty Space*, appeared in 1968, and he has since published *The Shifting Point* (1987), *There are No Secrets* (1993), and his autobiography *Threads of Time* (1998).

Also in the Dramatic Contexts series

Peter Brook

Evoking Shakespeare

Nick Hern Books

London

A Nick Hern Book

Evoking Shakespeare first published as a paperback original in Great Britain in 1998 by Nick Hern Books Limited, 14 Larden Road, London W3 7ST

A CIP catalogue record for this book is available from the British Library

ISBN 1 85459 303 X

Typeset by Country Setting, Kingsdown, Kent CT14 8ES

Printed and bound in Great Britain by Cox and Wyman, Reading, Berks

Evoking Shakespeare

Evoking Shakespeare

You pick up a newspaper – you think it's today's paper – and you read it with interest. Then suddenly you realise that this is yesterday's paper, and it's of no interest at all. Why is this? The men and women who put the paper together are undoubtedly intelligent, they write well, yet what they have written is ninety per cent dead the next day and the newspaper is only good to wrap up fish. What then is the difference between a page of yesterday's paper and a page of Shakespeare written hundreds of years ago? Why is Shakespeare not out of date? This sounds like a frivolous, easy question. But in fact, if you think of it, the easy answers can't satisfy any of us. Because what would be the easy answer? For instance, 'Shakespeare was a genius.' What understanding can we get from the word 'a genius'? Or else, 'Shakespeare was a great man of his time.' What does that help us to understand? Or else, to take the answers that the contemporary school of criticism might give: 'Shakespeare was more interested in going to bed with a boy than with a woman.' Does that in any way open up to us the true mystery of the phenomenon of Shakespeare? You will all remember that not so long ago people were seriously trying to discover whether Shakespeare really existed, and there were many theories over the last hundred years which put other names in the place of 'Shakespeare' – Bacon, Marlowe, Oxford, etc. The absurdity of this is that, again, it doesn't help us. You change the name, that's all. The mystery remains . . .

I went to Russia recently, and somebody stood up in an audience and said: 'We all know here that Shakespeare came from Uzbekistan because the name "Sheik" is an Arab term and a "peer" is a wise man, so "Shakespeare" was a code name to tell everyone that he was a Crypto-Moslem living in a Protestant country where Catholics were being persecuted.' Again, does this help us to enter into the Shakespeare enigma? Was Chekhov a Czech? There was another snobbish, racist view that was current for a long time in England, which held that as Shakespeare came from the country and was a poor boy who went to the local school, he was incapable of reaching the level of education that his plays reveal. In fact I think he was about twenty-eight when he wrote his first play. If you think of the capacity for assimilation of words, of impressions, of all the young people today who are making films at the age of twenty and twenty-one, if you think that Shakespeare was living in a period when there was a coming and going across London of people from all parts of the world, there is one thing that one can, I think, assume as a fact. That is that to be able to write his plays, Shakespeare must have had an extraordinary memory. Let us start from here.

*U*ndoubtedly, Shakespeare was genetically endowed with an extraordinary capacity to observe, an extraordinary capacity to assimilate and an extraordinary capacity to remember. I was talking about this the other day with a young conductor, about the possibility, even when one is very young, to record in one's brain a complex score. It's clear that that was one of Shakespeare's extraordinary capacities.

*D*on't forget that he lived in a very, very active and busy city which was London at the time, where it was sufficient to go into any bar to hear conversations between people who had crossed the seas from all parts of the world. So his ears absorbed an extraordinary variety of information.

Genetically speaking, Shakespeare was a phenomenon, and the bald head we have seen on so many pictures had an amazing, computer-like capacity for registering and processing a tremendously rich variety of impressions. This is the Shakespeare brain, the Shakespeare instrument, and it is also, I think, our starting point. Now, is it sufficient to say he had a great memory? I don't think so. For even if he could allow impressions to enter into his brain in all their richness, in all their complexity, that still would not be enough to make of him Shakespeare the unique dramatist. So, we are forced to conclude that another fundamental characteristic was there in him. We could call it 'creativity'. But even then where does that word lead us, what does it explain? Let's be very simple. We can say he was a poet and nobody can contradict us — because, after all, he wrote poetry. However, being a poet comes from somewhere. What, in fact, in concrete terms, is the ground out of which this particular thing called 'poetry' arises? A feeling for words, yes — a love of literary expression, yes, but that is not enough. We are looking for something very very fundamental.

What is fundamental is that a poet is a human being like every one of us — with a difference. The difference is that we, at any given moment, don't have access to the whole of our lives. Just look at ourselves now. At this very moment, as we are sitting here together. None of us is capable of penetrating below the conscious level of his or her listening, to enter into the entire richness of what we have absorbed over our whole life. In many of us, it could take a long search to dig into our past impressions. For some of us it would even need years with a psychiatrist to reach into those strange tunnels where all one's experiences are buried waiting to be revived. But a poet is different. The absolute characteristic of 'being a poet' is the capacity to see connections where, normally, connections are not obvious.

T. S. Eliot describes this in relation to coffee spoons – 'I've measured out my life in coffee spoons'. The coffee spoon at one and the same time evokes the human associations that are personal to the poet, and which also reach out far beyond the personal. Now let's return to Shakespeare and stay very close to indisputable facts. When Shakespeare wrote his plays, we have every reason to believe that he wrote fast. He was a practical man, who was writing in a practical theatre for productions that had to go on constantly; and, if you look at his output and the amount of years that it covers, he must have written at great speed. We've got no reason to believe that he was the sort of author who wrote a draft, put it away, then twenty years later took it out of his drawer and reworked it. Everything suggests that there weren't drafts; there's no record of drafts of Shakespeare's plays being found, nor of manuscripts that were not used. Everything suggests the opposite — that the most extraordinary of his plays were written in the heat of the moment, with a burning passion to put down exactly what he was imagining.

*H*e always began to write a play with a story. And here, I think, we can see the differences between the writer in the newspaper – the good writer in the Morgenpost – and Shakespeare. If you are writing the story of a crime for a newspaper, you write in a concise way, you write on one level, you only describe the surface of the action. Shakespeare had the greatest respect for story-telling, but he did something totally different. At each second he was conscious not only of the action itself, but also of the relationships on an infinite number of levels that were connected to that action. So he was forced to develop for himself a very extraordinary and complex instrument which we call 'poetry', by which within one single line he could give both the narrative meaning – which

has to be there, the human character
meaning which has to be there — and at
the same time find the appropriate words
amongst the twenty thousand English
words that were at his disposal: find
the words that contain the resonances,
that bring together all the different
levels of association that he was
carrying within him.

Then there is another aspect to this
phenomenon. A play of Shakespeare's
is not longer than any ordinary play,
a paragraph of the text is the same
length as the ordinary paragraph in
today's newspaper; but the density —
the density of the moment — is where
the whole interest for us lies. This
density involves many elements, and
one of the most important is the
imagery: but there are also the words,

and then the words take on extraordinary dimensions through the fact
that the words are not just 'concepts'.

*E*ven if a concept is something necessary in speech, it is a tragically pathetic
portion of the amazing whole that
speech can offer. Concept is that little
thin intellectual strain that the whole
of western civilisation has bowed down
to excessively for so many centuries.
Concept is there, but beyond concept is
the 'concept brought into life by image',
and beyond concept and image is music
– and word music is the expression of
what cannot be caught in conceptual
speech. Human experience that cannot
be conceptualized is expressed through
music. Poetry comes out of this,
because in poetry you have an infinitely
subtle relationship between rhythm,

tone, vibration and energy, which give
to each word as it is spoken concept,
image and at the same time an infinitely
powerful further dimension which comes
from sound, from the verbal music. And
yet, I think how dangerous it is even to
mention the word 'music'. This can
lead to a terrifying misunderstanding.
An actor can take this to mean, 'Ah!
I have a musical voice so I can speak
musically'. Let's be clear. Word music
in the poetic sense is something very
subtle; word rhythm is something very
subtle; but tragically in theatre schools
all over the world this has been reduced
to a set of rules. If actors are taught
that Shakespeare wrote in pentameters,
and the pentameters have a certain beat,
and the actors try to use this in their
speech, you get a dry, empty music,
which is not the living music that is
there in the words.

So let's come back to the central questions. What is the life within these plays? What, in fact, is the Shakespeare phenomenon? Shakespeare wrote, I think, thirty-seven plays. Within these plays, there must have been about a thousand characters. That means that in his plays Shakespeare himself – about whom we know so little – did something unique in the history of all writing. He managed moment after moment to enter into at least one thousand shifting points of view. So now it must be clear that the moment one tries to reduce Shakespeare in any way to any single viewpoint one is doing oneself a great disservice. If you say Shakespeare was a fascist – indeed there are books on the subject which say 'Shakespeare was a fascist', and there are productions of *Coriolanus* to prove that Shakespeare hated the people and was a fascist – or else *The Merchant of Venice* shows that Shakespeare was anti-semitic – all these narrow-minded misunderstandings are based on seizing one portion of one play and saying: 'Ah, now we know why the play was written.' The result of this approach today is above all sexual: we witness every sort of sexual interpretation of a play in attempts to prove that the play was written to reveal this or that sexual hidden relationship. Take a step back and look more broadly, more generously, and you see that Shakespeare has equal compassion and equal identification with all these shifting and changing attitudes, and he puts them all the time one in front of the other. At that point you find that it is almost impossible to discover a Shakespeare point of view, unless you say that being Shakespeare

21

he contained in himself at least a thousand Shakespeares. But why is this important for us to understand?

Consider the form of theatre that Shakespeare entered into. It was already very exciting and vibrant – the Elizabethan playhouse had the same excitement as the cinema had twenty to thirty years ago – the cinema in which Orson Welles made *Citizen Kane* was a cinema in which a whole new world of possibilities was opened. Now this new form of theatre was a theatre that was based on a platform – roughly like this one where I am standing – on which imagery could come and go. As there was no scenery, if someone said, 'We are in a forest', we were in a forest, and the next second if they said, 'We are not in the forest', the forest had vanished. That technique is faster than a cut in the cinema. In a film, you have the total picture of a forest — cut — to a total picture of, say, Berlin; but these are two separate things. When this is evoked by an actor with words it's much quicker, because the actor, as he is saying 'forest', can, within the same line of verse, make the forest — and Berlin — and you and me — appear — disappear — show you already a big close-up of a face, go into a heart, and the forest can reappear and go away again. This fluidity is beyond any form of film technique that's yet been invented.

*T*he architecture of the playhouse helped this greatly. Shakespeare's platform was a structure with different levels. There was a level up here, and

there was still another level higher up
that was used from time to time. And
now as I talk I realise that I am about
to say something that terrifies people
today here in Berlin. I don't know if
I dare to mention the word which,
when I used it here about ten years ago,
sent a feeling of horror through the
entire audience. The word was 'metaphysical'. Ten years ago in the political
climate of Berlin, the only thing that
mattered was a strict political point
of view on this and that, and anything
that went beyond that was weak and
old-fashioned and soft at the edges.
You must tell me whether times change,
whether the word 'metaphysics' is
less poisonous and dangerous. But you
can be certain that for Shakespeare
and for his audience, and for the time
in which he was living, with the
tremendous mixture of people in

transformation, with ideas exploding and collapsing, there was a lack of complete security. This was a blessing because it created a very deep intuitive sense that behind this chaos there was some strange possibility of under- standing, related to another sort of order, an order that had nothing to do with political order. That meaning is present through all the plays of Shakespeare, and – as Gordon Craig wrote a hundred years ago – if one refuses to accept the reality of a world of spirits it's much better to burn all the works of Shakespeare because they don't have any meaning at all any more. Shakespeare's theatre was a meeting- place between audience and players, in which scenes of life could be seen with great intensity, second by second.

*E*very visible dimension was
accompanied by its invisible dimension,
and that's why the action took place
horizontally and vertically throughout
all Shakespeare's plays. Now one can
begin to see how it is that his form
of writing had to be so compact and
so dense. Also, I think one can see
something else if one makes, just for
a moment, this obvious relationship
between his stage and today's cinema.
Not because there was a freedom to
have big scenes and small scenes, and
battle scenes and spectacles – that's
obvious. Something quite different.
I don't know if it's ever struck you as
strongly as it's always struck me that
the cinema has developed a very, very
complex artificial language which
everyone can understand. One minute
you have a long shot, next minute you

have a close shot, next you are somewhere else, and this very complex
syntax is crystal-clear all over the world
to people of every culture, every back-
ground, and one can say every level of
education. Gordon Craig, whom I knew
when he was about ninety, said to me:
'I can't go to the cinema.' I said: 'Why
not?' 'When I am sitting there', he said,
'and one minute I am looking at the
picture of a mountain, then suddenly it
jumps and there is a big face right in
front of me, I can't understand
anything at all.'

Now he – Gordon Craig – was unique
and his points of view were always
eccentric, but he expressed truly what a
strange language the cinema was
developing. However, he was alone in
his reaction, and almost all the entire

rest of humanity without difficulty
followed long shot, cut, close shot, cut,
tracking shot, as a simple and natural
language. Now, in the Elizabethan
theatre, exactly the same thing
happened with poetry. An extremely
complicated form evolved itself in
which at one moment somebody is
speaking to someone else in a natural
everyday way, and yet, two words later,
they are using expressions that you
would never, ever, use in a normal
conversation. And he wrote strange
adjectives, and used sudden jolts in
rhythm that could never occur in life.
Or within the phrases suddenly there is
a philosophical inquiry, a metaphysical
riddle that could never appear between
two people chatting together.
Now from one point of view this is an
artificial language, an artificial language
for connoisseurs, but for the

Elizabethan audience there was no problem: as for filmgoers today, it seemed completely natural – natural because it was necessary. The audience sitting there was not composed of intellectuals saying: 'Ah, this is a triumph of style', or arguing: 'What is the stylistic reason behind this?' When Shakespeare's plays were put on for the big popular audience, we have no evidence to suggest that anyone found this unfolding structure of words in any way unusual. It was many hundred years before someone would begin to say: 'Ah, I love going to the theatre, because I love its "artificiality".' 'Artificiality' only entered the theatre after Shakespeare's time, with scenery, make-up, *trompe l'oeil*, *chiaroscuro*, and then what are called 'theatre lovers' began to say: 'I love the artificiality of the stage.' But in fact, in Shakespeare's open arena, with the people standing around a platform, everything, whether natural or unnatural, seemed just like life.

*W*hen Shakespeare wrote: 'I am holding a mirror – we hold a mirror up to nature' – what this implies is that human beings within human life are being reflected. But that doesn't mean that they are reflected naturalistically, like in real life, not even artificially. When on my way here I saw a sign saying 'Kultur ist heute', the word 'Kultur' filled me with horror because 'Kultur' can easily lead one to believe: 'If it's artificial – ah, then it's culture!' No. A true mirror of life is never cultural, never artificial, it reflects what is there. And a theatre does not only show the surface, it shows what is hidden behind the surface, in the intricate social interrelations of the people and, behind that, what is the ultimate existential meaning of this activity called life – all of these go together, and are shown in the great mirror. But to show the whole of life in this way is an incredible task, and it demands a form that is extraordinarily compact which is why I come back to the same point. Moment by moment the material is of such enormous density that it demands every resource that language has to offer. This means poetry. Not poetry as prettiness but poetry as compactness, poetry as language charged with intensity.

*L*et's now come back to our real difficulty, to the present. Today we see that if we try to stage a play of Shakespeare, the challenge is to help

the audience to look and listen with the
eyes and ears of the present. What we
look at must seem natural now, today.
'Seem natural' means that we don't put
into question what we see. If you once
think, 'Is this natural or unnatural?'
you're kaputt. An actor is speaking
and taking a glass of water, this is
natural, and at that moment that
person goes into poetry, into very
complex speech – that must also seem
natural – and if they do a strange
movement, that must be natural too.
In other words, the problem is adapting
this material to the present moment,
the present moment being now – the
moment when people are sitting here in
the audience.

*B*ut there's a trap. 'The present'
and 'contemporary' are not the same

thing. A director can take any play
of Shakespeare and can make it contemporary in the simplest, crudest way.
For instance, you can have people
coming on stage with guns and riding
motorbikes, and they shit on stage.
There are a hundred ways in which you
can bring something into the recognis-
able present. As a director you are free,
but this freedom brings you unavoid-
ably against a tough and painful
question. It obliges you to be deeply
respectful, sensitive and open as you
explore the text. You have to ask
yourself as director: are you in touch
with all the levels of the writing which
are rich, fruitful and meaningful and
life-giving as much today as in the past,
or are you saying either I haven't
noticed these levels, or they are not
interesting, or just I don't care? You can
do what you want — but one must

recognise the gap between a crude
modernising of a text and the amazing
potential within it that is being
ignored. And as there are so few
potentials in the theatre of this quality,
then one must recognise that one is
taking a risk which perhaps is not
worth taking. To sum up. The article
in yesterday's newspaper has only one
dimension and it fades fast. Each line
in Shakespeare is an atom. The energy
that can be released is infinite – if we
can split it open.

Q *It seems that you work in Paris of your own free will and that usually means, as with* Qui est là, *that you are doing Shakespeare in French. How many of these levels that you've been describing actually suffer in working with Shakespeare in a foreign language or are there some advantages to that?*

A very interesting question, because the plays don't suffer, but I do. For an Englishman it is a real suffering. Because the moment you translate, one level of the music goes. What is extraordinary about Shakespeare is that there is so much in his plays that even when you take away what with most poetic writers would be ninety per cent of their true value, an extraordinary and magnificent material remains. With Shakespeare the mysterious power is there even in translation, out of which comes the energy that can lead to performance. It is there in the characters, in their relations, in all the other aspects, and also in the ideas that are within his language – all of that leaves something tremendous even when this magical level of the words is diminished. And of course it's very interesting in exchange to work with translators and to see – for instance in French – the problem is very interesting, because in French you have the language which is perhaps the farthest removed from English, it's a completely different way of thought and way of expression.

*A*nd a complicated phrase with strange adjectives, which seems completely natural in English, if it is translated very faithfully into French, becomes extraordinarily artificial, pompous and flowery. So the French translator has to make a choice and simplify the line to rediscover its purity, at the expense of sacrificing some of what in English is part of its real value.

Q *Is there a special way in which Shakespeare is dealing with violence, destruction, negative aspects of life, and is this way still concerning us?*

I have just been working on a play of Beckett and the same question is always asked. Is he pessimistic, is he optimistic, should we be pessimistic, should we be optimistic today? And, you see, these are all politicians' lies. Optimism in front of reality is a lie, pessimism is a masturbation and a self-indulgence. But the third attitude

is extraordinarily difficult because it
means opening oneself to what is
intolerable in human existence and
what, on the contrary, is radiant in
human existence – simultaneously.
Now, the reason, when some years ago
we spent a long time working on the
Mahabharata, was that the *Mahabharata*
is about war, about violence, about all
the themes that are in the present-day
cinema. And at the same time the
deepest meaning of conflict in the
human pattern is explored in a way that
is very different from a film about the
horror of war. It can lead us into feeling
more alive rather than more suicidal,
and I think that this really is the
quality that you find in Greek tragedy,
where the worse the events, the truer
you know them to be. And yet the truer
you know them to be the more
inevitable you see them to be, and the

more the reaction for yourself in an audience is neither complacent, nor suicidal. Curiously, this intensifies your capacity to live. And this seems to me present in the whole work of Shakespeare. For instance, you take *King Lear*. Nowhere in *King Lear* can you find anyone closing their eyes to the cruelty of mankind, and yet the play is not a black existentialist play showing that mankind is a worthless species, nor a naive expression that all mankind is noble and beautiful. The vertical and the horizontal are there at one and the same time to be grasped if one wants to and if one can.

Q *Why do you relate this capacity – memory – of Shakespeare to his genes?*

I think – perhaps you don't agree – that a prodigious memory and a capacity to listen and observe are part of the inborn qualities of a human being. And what is interesting is to see the use that's made of them. And there one can see that Shakespeare, from his first play to his last, lived very actively and very intensively with his own life experiences. The potential was obviously there when he was born and when he first put pen to paper, with his first play. But at the moment when he wrote his first play he hadn't lived the human experiences and the human interrogations that led him later to be able to write *Hamlet*, and write *King Lear*, and eventually to write *The Tempest*. So that one sees a very interesting relationship between what's inborn and what is developed by life.

Q   *What can one understand in* Hamlet *in relation to a metaphysical level?*

I think that in *Hamlet*, perhaps of all plays, this is very simple, because if you take the ghost out of *Hamlet* it's no longer the same story. If you take the spirits out of the *Midsummer Night's Dream*, it's no longer the same story. You can make other stories about a man killed by his brother or a son becoming suspicious and deciding to revenge himself on his uncle — but that's not *Hamlet*. In *Hamlet* the shock that is brought to a young man is because he actually sees his father's ghost, and through the father's ghost he learns that the father has been murdered. One of the questions that run through the play is: 'Is this an illusion?' The word 'illusion' is there from the start. Is this an illusion or is this a reality? Now, one doesn't have to go further than that to see that somebody who is tormented by that question is forced to enquire into every aspect of life. He questions his relations with women, he doubts the purity of a woman who at the same time seems crystal-clear and totally honest. What does this mean? Is this mysterious figure saying, 'You must kill' an authority to be respected or not? These are not simple questions, but they are all brought into existence by the spirit, in a way that in the *Midsummer Night's Dream* the whole question of love becomes concrete because of an interplay between physical love and other levels incarnated by spirits. And the same goes for *The Tempest*: I wrote down this morning something which I think is interesting because it touches on this question of the different levels of Shakespeare. These are the last words of *The Tempest*, maybe the last words Shakespeare ever wrote. And it's interesting if one listens to them, from the point of view of an actor who is trying to understand what in fact the character of Prospero could be.

> *My ending is despair*
> *Unless it be relieved by prayer*
> *Which pierces so that it assaults*
> *Mercy itself and frees all faults.*
> *As you from crimes would pardon'd be*
> *Let your indulgence set me free.*

It's interesting for us to look at this in detail because within this one can see both the possibilities and the difficulties that are there all through Shakespeare's works.

The first phrase is very simple and introduces a theme that everyone can understand on its first level:

> *My ending is despair*
> *Unless it be relieved by prayer*

But if you take it in isolation, the thought is banal. Listen: despair and prayer rhyme. In any little English boarding house you could see this written on the wall on a little card saying, 'My ending is despair unless it is relieved by prayer.' If the actor says it like a homely motto, he is ignoring the fact that the word is not 'by prayer' but 'by prayer which' and 'which' is a moment of suspense. What follows the 'which'?

> *Which pierces so that it assaults*
> *Mercy itself*

Next comes 'assaults', and you can always see in Shakespeare's writing that, as he writes, when his hand comes back to the beginning of a new line there is always a special force. You feel it in the actual texture of the writing of his verse that the end of a phrase is like an upbeat in music that's leading to – what? – suspense. And the word that follows is 'mercy'. Now can we understand a prayer that not only 'penetrates' but also can 'assault' mercy? So the idea of assault is extraordinary – there is a power in the words themselves, they are very unusual words – 'I assault mercy.' A prayer assaults mercy. There is something tremendously powerful not only in the words but in the image, the image of something abstract and vast called mercy being assaulted like a citadel.

I am trying to open up for you the fact that we are in front of something, which we cannot ever finally understand. Now this is very important, because the whole of work in Shakespeare production and Shakespeare acting turns around the question of when you

have the right to be absolutely sure and when, on the contrary, your only true position is one of open questioning.
I don't know if we have any cardinals or high theological authorities in the audience today, but personally I don't believe that there is a theological authority today who can tell us with absolute certainty what it means to say: 'a prayer which pierces so that it assaults mercy.' I think this is deliberately written by a poet not to encapsulate an understanding but to open a burning mystery. And you see that it carries on by saying that if that incomprehensible act happens, it leads to freedom.

> *and frees all faults.*
> *As you from crimes would pardon'd be*

– very strong word 'crimes' –

> *Let your indulgence set me free.*

So if you now look at this incredible complexity of writing, written — I am sure — in the heat of the moment, you can draw out of this a chain, and the chain is: despair — prayer — assault — mercy — crime — pardon — indulgence — free. If an actor or if a director take this to be just a happy ending you can say they haven't bothered to listen to the words.

*I*f you think in terms of clichés and decide that Shakespeare wrote the play just as a piece about colonialism, then you are refusing to see that what leads to the last word 'free' concerns the meaning of freedom in all its dimensions and implications.

*N*one of the words we just quoted stands in isolation. The passage leads

inexorably to the last word of all, and
the questions it evokes are truly for
today wherever they are spoken. Always
the closer one comes in contact with
the Shakespearean material, the more
this is a meeting point between living
material and ourselves and is never just
the expression of his point of view. And
the words only come into new life when
once again they become the meeting
point with people of today, whether
they are actors, directors or spectators.
With the purpose of leaving us in front
of open questions which we must struggle
with once again – for ourselves.

*A*fter which I must quote Shakespeare
and ask you with your indulgence to set
me free.

Berlin, 12 May 1996